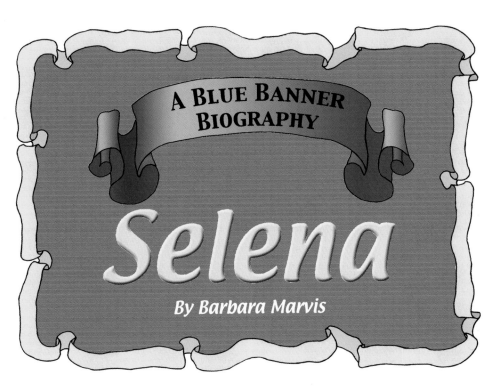

A BLUE BANNER
BIOGRAPHY

Selena

By Barbara Marvis

Mitchell Lane
PUBLISHERS

P.O. Box 196
Hockessin, Delaware 19707
Visit us on the web: www.mitchelllane.com
Comments? email us: mitchelllane@mitchelllane.com

Printing   3   4   5   6   7   8   9

Blue Banner Biographies

Alicia Keys	Allen Iverson	Avril Lavigne
Beyoncé	Bow Wow	Britney Spears
Christina Aguilera	Christopher Paul Curtis	Clay Aiken
Condoleezza Rice	Daniel Radcliffe	Derek Jeter
Eminem	Eve	Ja Rule
Jay-Z	Jennifer Lopez	J.K. Rowling
Jodie Foster	Lance Armstrong	Mary-Kate and Ashley Olsen
Melissa Gilbert	Michael Jackson	Missy Elliott
Nelly	P. Diddy	Queen Latifah
Rita Williams-Garcia	Ritchie Valens	Ron Howard
Rudy Giuliani	Sally Field	**Selena**
Shirley Temple		

Library of Congress Cataloging-in-Publication Data
Marvis, Barbara J.
    Selena/Barbara Marvis.
        p. cm. — (A blue banner biography)
    Summary: Looks at the life and career of Selena, the award-winning Tejano singer who was shot and killed by the president of her fan club in a dispute over finances.
    Includes bibliographical references (p.) and index.
    Discography: p.
    ISBN 1-58415-226-5 (library bound)
    1. Selena, 1971-1995—Juvenile literature. 2. Tejano musicians—Biography—Juvenile literature. [1. Selena, 1971-1995. 2. Singers. 3. Mexican Americans—Biography. 4. Women—Biography. 5. Tejano music.] I. Title. II. Series.
    ML3930.S43M371 2003
    782.42164—dc21   2003008855

ABOUT THE AUTHOR: Barbara Marvis has been a writer for more than twenty-five years. She is the author of the successful series, *Famous People of Hispanic Heritage*. She has written several other books for young adults including *Tommy Nuñez: NBA Referee/Taking My Best Shot*. She holds a B.S. degree in English and communications from West Chester State University and an M.Ed. in remedial reading from the University of Delaware.
PHOTO CREDITS: Cover: Charles W. Bush/Shooting Star; p. 4 AP Photo; p. 13 Corbis; p. 19 AP Photo; p. 24 Corbis; p. 28 Getty Images; p. 29 AP Photo/Victoria Advocate
ACKNOWLEDGMENTS: The following story has been thoroughly researched, and to the best of our knowledge, represents a true story. While every possible effort has been made to ensure accuracy, the publisher will not assume liability for damages caused by inaccuracies in the data, and makes no warranty on the accuracy of the information contained herein.

CONTENTS

When Selena died, her career was on the brink of international success.

Young Selena

On March 30, 1995, Marcela Quintanilla received a phone call from her daughter, Selena. "Mom," she said, "let's go have lunch."

"My foot was swollen," remembers Mrs. Quintanilla. "I'd broken my ankle, but I wanted to spend the time with her. I'm so glad I went. We sat in this restaurant for about four hours, and she told me about another time she'd eaten there. A little old lady was eating by herself. Selena felt bad for her so she told the waiter she wanted to pay for the lady's meal, but not to say who did it. Later, Selena called the waiter over and said, 'I want you to give her one of those little cakes you give people on their birthdays. Put it in a bag so she can take it home.' When she told me this story, I wanted to cry. Then Selena drove me home. She was weaving in and out of traffic and singing. I grabbed her ear and said, 'I love you.' And she said, 'I love you, Mama.' When we got back, she came in and talked to her father for a few minutes. Then she said, 'I've got to get home to my husband — he's waiting for me.' She left. And I didn't see her again."

The very next day, Selena was shot to death by her fan-club president and boutique manager, Yolanda Saldívar, in a dispute over missing funds. The beautiful Tejano singer was just two weeks shy of her twenty-fourth birthday and two days short of her third wedding anniversary to Chris Pérez, her band's guitarist. Her tragic death cut short a career that was on the brink of international success.

The Quintanilla family has lived and worked in Texas for at least a hundred years.

Selena Quintanilla was born on April 16, 1971, in Lake Jackson, Texas, a small town seventy-five miles southwest of Houston. She was the youngest of three children born to Marcela and Abraham Quintanilla, Jr. Selena had an older brother, Abraham III (A.B.), who was eight years her senior, and a sister, Suzette, who was four years older than she.

The Quintanilla family has lived and worked in Texas for at least a hundred years. They are of Mexican ancestry. Selena's great grandfather, Eulojio Quintanilla, was born in northern Mexico in 1886 and came to Texas not long after. His wife, Doloris (Selena's great grandmother), was born in the United States in 1892.

Selena spent her early childhood in Lake Jackson, which is one of nine small towns on the flat coastal plains of Brazoria County. Though commercial fishing also supports the town, chemicals are the mainstay of the economy there. Abraham Quintanilla worked for Dow Chemical as a shipping clerk in those early years. But his real passion had always been music. According to his brother, Eddie Quintanilla, Abraham loved street-corner doo-wop music and rhythm and blues, but he played traditional Tex-Mex music — polkas and waltzes with Spanish music — when he was in high school (1950s) with a band he belonged to called *Los Dinos* (The Boys). He was the vocalist. Abraham recognized Selena's musical talents when she was quite young.

Selena's father recognized her musical talents when she was quite young.

One day, when Selena was just five, her father was playing the guitar in their home. Selena came over to his knee and began to sing. Her voice was pure and her pitch was perfect. "I could see it from day one," her father said. "She loved all music." So Abraham soundproofed his garage and began teaching his children about the music he loved so much. They formed a little band they called *Selena y Los Dinos* after Abraham's high-school band. A.B. was on bass, Suzette played drums, and Selena sang. They also included two other children in their band:

Rodney Pyeatt and Rena Dearman. Before long, they were playing at weddings and parties.

Selena attended first grade at Oran M. Roberts Elementary School. The students there were from all over Latin America, and also included Anglo-Americans and African-Americans. Many of her classmates were from Chile and Argentina. Their parents had come to Dow Chemical through a special training program.

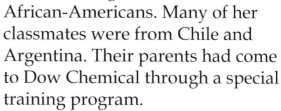

The whole family pitched in to make Abraham's restaurant business work.

Selena's first-grade teacher, Nina McGlashan, remembers Selena very clearly. "She tried really hard at whatever she was doing and was eager to learn—just the kind of student you always like to have. What I remember is that big smile. Selena had a real perky personality. She participated in everything. She was easy to get along with and very well liked by the other children."

In 1980, Abraham Quintanilla quit his job at Dow Chemical to start his own Tex-Mex restaurant, which he called Papagallo's. The whole family pitched in to help make it work. All the children had chores at the struggling restaurant. On most weekends, their band performed. But despite how hard they worked, the restaurant went under only one year later. The area was caught in a recession caused by the Texas oil bust, and people stopped going out to eat. As a result of the restaurant failure, the Quintanillas lost their home, many of their possessions, and, above all, their livelihood. In 1981, when Selena was only nine, the family moved to Corpus Christi, where they started their musical career out of necessity. "We had no alternative," Selena recalled in a 1992 interview.

The family made music their full-time career as they traveled across Texas and the United States in a battered van pulling a broken-down trailer. They mostly toured the back country of South Texas, playing everywhere from wedding halls to honky-tonks. "If we got ten people in one place, that was great," said Selena. "We ate a lot of hamburgers and shared everything."

Selena's father managed the band. He thought they would be most successful going the Tejano route. Tejano is a lively Spanish-language blend of Tex-Mex rhythms, pop-style tunes, and German polka that was not all that popular at the time. The only problem was, Selena didn't speak any Spanish. Selena had been raised to speak only English at home and at school. Her father had to teach her Spanish phonetically; it was through music that Selena learned to speak Spanish.

Selena's family started their musical career once the restaurant went under. They had no choice.

In Corpus Christi, Selena attended West Oso Junior High School. She was an excellent student, but she was forced to stop going when she was in eighth grade, because she was on the road so much with her family. She did continue her schooling through home school courses and went on to earn her equivalency degree. Selena felt she missed most of her teen years because she could not attend school, and she later became an advocate of all children completing their high-school education. She felt she had many life experiences during her teen years, however, that made her seem far more mature than her years. Selena made her first commercial recording in 1985, for a small Texas label (San Antonio-based Manny Guerra), when she was just fourteen years old.

> *Selena's teenage experiences made her seem far more mature than her years.*

While the Quintanillas were on the road, they frequently ran into another traveling bandsman at dances, weddings, and other festivals. His name was Johnny Canales. Johnny knew Abraham from their days in high school, when they both had bands. Later, Johnny would host his own international Spanish-language television program, *The Johnny Canales Show*. When Selena was twelve or thirteen, she first performed on Johnny's show, and she appeared about a dozen more times over the years.

"When she was young and starting out, our show was small, about five TV stations," Johnny remembers. "Over the years, as [Selena] grew, we did, too. It's like we've grown up together." A lot of people knew Selena from her appearances on *The Johnny Canales Show*. She became an instant hit just as the show was beginning to be a big hit as well. *The Johnny Canales Show* was broadcast internationally on the Univision network, bringing Tejano music into twenty-three countries, over five hundred stations, in nearly two hundred markets.

Johnny Canales remembers when he first realized that Selena was headed for stardom. "We took her across the border to Matamoros in 1986, and I was dying to see how the Mexican people would react. She took the stage and they went wild."

But even as recently as 1988, the family didn't make very much money. "In 1988, the family was playing in Idaho, and they were staying in a small hotel because money was still tight," Johnny recalls. "The Quintanillas had just purchased an old over-the-road coach. There were seats in the front and mattresses laid out in back. At the end of their show, Selena was sitting in the front seat eating a late dinner of potted meat and weenies. I said, 'Selena, are you still eating that stuff?' and she said, 'Yes, I don't want to get used to the good life.'"

In 1988, the family still wasn't making very much money. They had an old coach with mattresses in the back.

Rising Star

When *Selena y Los Dinos* was just starting out, Tejano music was not very popular in Mexico. It was nearly forbidden in Puerto Rico and the Puerto Rican neighborhoods of New York City. It was shunned in Florida. That is, until they heard Selena.

Selena's lifelong ambition was to take her music across all racial, cultural, and economic barriers. This was not an easy task. Selena was part of the Tejano culture. The Tejano music was in her blood. The Tejanos were originally Mexican-Americans who were born or lived in Texas. They experienced a difficult type of prejudice that many other Latino groups in America did not even know existed. The Anglo-Texans often discriminated against them, and though it is not a constant problem today, there are still open incidents of ethnic bias. The Mexicans (on the other side of the border) often held many prejudices against the Tejanos as well. Most young Tejanos speak and read only

English, and, according to many Mexicans, none of the Tejanos speaks Spanish correctly. The Tejanos even refer to their language as "Spanglish." Selena wanted her music to moderate the ethnic prejudice many in Texas felt.

As the band received increasing recognition, Selena's father continued to do all he could to support his rising star. He managed the band, handled the bookings, worked the sound boards, and collected the money. In 1987, Selena won the Tejano Music Awards in San Antonio for female vocalist and performer of the year. This was a big break for the Quintanillas, who had graduated to singing in ballrooms and cut nearly a dozen albums for their regional label. In 1989, Abraham signed a breakthrough six-figure deal for the band to cut Spanish-language records for EMI's new Latin division. The old tour coach was replaced with the most modern Silver Eagle coaches: one bus for the

Selena's dream was to have her music heard all over the world.

Quintanilla family and one for the band. There were six increasingly successful albums, topped by *Selena Live!*, which received a Grammy in 1994 for the best Mexican-American performance, then her last complete album, *Amor Prohibido* (Forbidden Love), which was nominated for a Grammy and sold over 500,000 copies. Selena was a total package: she was smart, she was beautiful, she could sing, and she could move. She was a millionaire by the time she was 19. At 21, she drew a crowd of 20,000 people to the fairgrounds in Pasadena, Texas. In 1994, 60,000 people showed up to hear her sing in Houston. It was not long before she moved to the big time. Later in 1994, the band received an English-language contract from SBK records (a division of EMI), and Selena was set to record her first all-English album that would bring her her dream and cross her over to mainstream America. She was on the road to international stardom. The album was to be released in mid-1995.

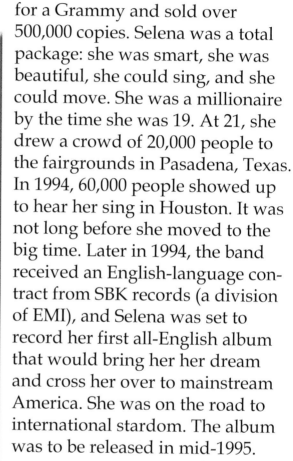

Selena was a total package: she was smart, she was beautiful, she could sing, and she could move.

Love and Stardom

Selena met Chris Pérez in 1988 when she went to San Antonio to attend a rehearsal of his band. He was twenty years old at the time, two years older than Selena. Chris joined *Selena y Los Dinos* as a guitarist in 1989, but it was not until 1991 that their romance began. For two years, they toured together as friends. Then one day, Selena's brother, A.B., hinted to Chris that Selena might be interested in being more than just friends. According to Chris, when he got the message, he realized his feelings were more than just friendship as well. They were in the Pizza Hut in Rio Grande Valley when Chris finally admitted to Selena that he would like their relationship to be something more. "I never wanted to see anyone else, I never went out with anyone else," Chris says. "It was just Selena and me." Selena told Chris she felt the same way and, little by little, it all came together. Chris and Selena were married on April 2, 1992. Friends and neighbors say they made a cute couple. Chris wore a short ponytail, which they found acceptable for a musician, and they saw him as an attentive, doting husband. The two were always holding hands.

Though her career advanced rapidly in the 1990s, she and her family never left the modest Molina neighborhood of Corpus Christi where she was raised. Selena built three homes right next to each other. She and her husband lived in one house; her mother and father lived in the middle house; and A.B. and his wife, Vangie, lived on the other side. Except for the expensive Silver Eagle coaches, the only other sign of wealth in the neighborhood was the Porsche automobile that Selena drove. In 1995, Selena and Chris were designing a 10-bedroom home on 10 acres of land in town so that the couple could have some privacy. It was to be Selena's dream home.

Selena continued to become more and more popular. Fame and fortune did nothing, however, to change the little girl from Corpus Christi. Selena's personality did not change as she grew more famous. She still wanted to remember the people who had supported her singing all those years. "Everybody loved Selena," a neighbor says, "not only because of her beauty and talent, but because of the way she was. Though she was famous, she would act just like any other person. She shopped at Wal-Mart and

Fame and fortune did not change Selena. She still remembered all the people who had supported her singing all those years.

ate at Pizza Hut." Even Johnny Canales, who knew Selena from the time she was very young, said fame never changed her.

Selena's popularity in the music world gave rise to many other business ventures that the Quintanillas had only dreamed about before 1991. Suddenly there were hit records, albums, a Grammy, concert and nightclub appearances, product endorsements, two promising boutiques, and then a fan club.

Selena was seen in public a great deal, but her family tried to maintain her privacy. Her father was very protective, often ushering her through adoring crowds to keep her from getting knocked over. Other men in the family protected Selena when her father was not around. But as her fame grew, so did the number of her fans. She became exceptionally popular, especially in south Texas. Among her fans was a registered nurse from San Antonio. Her name was Yolanda Saldívar.

Selena was seen in public a great deal, but her family tried to maintain her privacy.

Yolanda

*I*n early 1991, Yolanda Saldívar began calling Abraham Quintanilla about forming a fan club for Selena. She left repeated messages for him. At first, Abraham did not return her calls. Eventually the family decided the fan club might be a good idea, and they spoke to Yolanda about it.

Yolanda came from a big family in San Antonio. She was a loner, she was very quiet, she had no friends, she never married, and she had no children. She lived in a modest house with her mother and was a nurse at nearby hospitals. Other than the fact that she was the aunt of one of Selena's childhood friends, no one in Selena's family knew anything about her. But she was so enthusiastic, and she idolized Selena so, that she soon won Selena's support. In 1991, Selena gave her the unpaid position of founding a fan club. Yolanda became a faithful supporter.

Shortly after Saldívar was hired, Selena raved about her to the press. "She's doing exceptionally well," she said.

"Fan clubs can ruin you if people get upset and turned off by them. But she's doing really good." Selena showed her friendship by showering Yolanda with gifts. Yolanda was crazy about cows, and Selena bought her an $800 rug with

Selena and Yolanda Saldívar speak at a party after the 1994 Tejano Music Awards

a cow on it. Then she bought her a cow phone. Yolanda seemed utterly devoted to Selena.

In August 1994, Selena rewarded Yolanda by moving her to a paid position. She put Yolanda in charge of her new business venture, and Yolanda quit her position as a nurse. Selena opened a boutique called Selena Etc., Inc. One shop was opened in Corpus Christi and another in San Antonio. The shops sold a line of fashions and jewelry designed by Selena, and they also had salons for hairstyling and manicures. Selena Etc. was also involved in selling its products to other stores. But it was not long before Yolanda began having problems with the other employees.

> *Selena's employees began to notice that Yolanda, Selena's fan club founder, was quickly taking over her life.*

Martin Gomez was hired by the family to help produce the fashion lines. The fashions were called Martin Gomez Designs for Selena. "From the beginning," said Gomez, "there was a lot of tension between Yolanda and me. She was mean and manipulative." In January 1995, Gomez quit out of frustration. "I told Selena I was afraid of Yolanda," he said. "She wouldn't let me talk to Selena anymore. She was too possessive."

Out of loyalty to Yolanda, Selena did nothing. But employees of the boutique and others close to Selena saw a problem arising. Yolanda quickly began to take over Selena's life. Soon she had built a protective shield between Selena and the public.

One day in late 1994, there was an important style show at which some of Selena's new fashions were being introduced. Some friends and customers showed up early at the hotel in Corpus Christi where the show was being held. Before the doors had opened, there was a line waiting to get in. In that line was longtime family friend Rosita Rodela.

Rosita tried to get in to see Selena and Abraham before the show, but Yolanda wouldn't let her. "You can't come in," Yolanda said sharply. "It isn't open yet. You have to get back." She was very rude.

Rosita was shocked because Yolanda's behavior was in such contrast to the warm, courteous nature of the entire Quintanilla family. "I told her I was a friend of the family and I was sure they would see me. I asked to go see Abraham."

"He's busy," Yolanda snapped. But just at that moment, Abraham walked by and saw Rosita. She asked him if they could chat, and he said sure. Yolanda's eyes pierced Rosita as she walked through the door.

Selena's employees took up a collection to buy her a custom-made ring for Christmas of 1994.

For Christmas in 1994, Selena's employees took up a collection to purchase a custom-made ring for her. The ring was a 14-carat gold and diamond ring with a white gold egg, encrusted with fifty-two small diamonds. While all the employees had contributed to buying the ring, it appears that Yolanda led Selena to believe it was a personal gift from her alone. It was later believed that Yolanda in fact pocketed the employees' money and charged the ring to one of Selena's credit cards.

In January of 1995, Abraham began hearing about problems with Yolanda and the fan club.

In late January, Abraham began hearing rumors about problems with the fan club. Several fans complained that they had sent in their $22 membership fee for the fan club but had not received the promised T-shirt, CD, or photograph. About the same time, other employees began to raise questions about Yolanda. They said it appeared that Yolanda had been taking money from the business. Some of the employees' paychecks bounced, and there were rumors that Yolanda had bought herself a new truck with company funds. Abraham decided to confront Yolanda about the accusations without telling Selena. Yolanda denied doing anything wrong.

In early March, some employees from the San Antonio boutique revealed to Selena that Yolanda appeared to be taking money from the store. Abraham, Selena, and her sister, Suzette, met with Yolanda and demanded a full accounting. Yolanda claimed there were people who just wanted to make her look bad.

Tragedy

*O*n March 13, after undergoing a background check, Yolanda Saldívar purchased a snub-nosed .38-caliber pistol from a San Antonio gun shop. Then she went to Monterrey, Mexico, where Selena was planning to open another boutique. She took all of Selena's business records with her. At some point during the trip, Selena called Yolanda and told her to bring the records back.

On March 30, Yolanda called Selena to tell her she had brought the financial records back to Corpus Christi. She told her she would discuss the matter with her, if she would come to the Days Inn, where Yolanda was staying. She told her to come alone. Instead, Chris accompanied Selena to the hotel. The two returned home later that day without all the documents. There were still bank statements missing.

On the morning of March 31, Selena left home at 9 A.M. Yolanda had asked her to go with her to Doctor's

Selena actually became much more famous after her death.

Regional Medical Center, claiming that she had been raped in Monterrey. When the medical tests came back inconclusive, Yolanda admitted she had made up the story. Selena and Yolanda went back to Room 158 at the Days Inn to get the missing records.

When Selena asked Yolanda for the bank statements, the two exchanged harsh words. Selena decided to end their professional relationship by firing her. Yolanda then demanded that Selena return the ring on her finger, which had been a Christmas gift from her employees. As Selena went to take the ring from her finger, Yolanda pulled out a gun.

A maid at the Days Inn saw Selena run from the room. Yolanda chased her and shot her in the back. The bullet entered her right shoulder and severed an artery. Selena stumbled into the motel office asking for help. The desk clerk called 911. The call came just before noon.

An ambulance arrived within three minutes and whisked Selena to Memorial Medical Center. The hospital notified Abraham that his daughter had been in an accident and they must come right away. The family thought she had been in a car wreck. It was not until they arrived at the hospital that they found out she had been shot. There was nothing more the doctors could do. Selena bled to death just after 1:00 P.M.

In the meantime, Yolanda Saldívar sat in her truck outside the Days Inn and held the police at bay for nine hours. Finally, she surrendered to police and was taken away to the Nueces County jail.

On April 3, 1995, Selena Quintanilla Pérez was buried in Corpus Christi. More than 30,000 people walked by her casket the day before to pay their last respects. Hundreds of vigils, candlelight marches, and memorial Masses were held for Selena in the days following her death. It was difficult for her family to grieve in such a public way. There were hundreds of news stories, television shows, and magazine articles about Selena. Ironically, she became much more famous after her death.

After being fired, Yolanda asked Selena to return her ring and then chased her and shot her in the back.

Remembering
Selena

After Selena died, sales of her last album, *Amor Prohibido*, almost tripled, reaching 1.5 million copies. Business boomed at her Corpus Christi boutique. EMI Records decided to take advantage of the publicity, and they quickly released *Dreaming of You*, an album that Selena was making at the time of her death. The album contains five songs in English that she had recorded for the album. That was all that had been cut. Using the latest technology, EMI was able to lift her Spanish vocals from a song that had been released years earlier and mix them with new vocals by the group Barrio Boyzz. In addition, they included several songs that Selena had just recorded for the movie *Don Juan DeMarco*, in which Selena had had a small part with a Mexican mariachi band. In fact, the movie was released just a few days after her death. (Its release date had been planned many months before.)

There is no doubt that Selena was on the brink of international stardom when she was murdered. The fact that her business has flourished after her death is testimony to that.

Selena still has millions of fans all around the globe. Many young girls in Texas want to be just like her. She was more than a singer; she was also like a big sister. Before her death, Selena visited schools in predominantly Mexican-American neighborhoods all over the United States. She would remind the kids to stay in school, to not use drugs, and to be careful about sex. She told the children it was all right to aspire to be singers, but they must get their education, too. Days after her death, the Texas legislature unanimously passed a resolution honoring Selena's accomplishments as a role model for the state's youth, including her work educating Latinos about the dangers of drugs and AIDS.

Senator Eddie Lucio (D-Brownsville) said, "We're going to think about her as years go by, and Selena will be eternally young in the hearts and souls of all of us."

Since her passing, her life has inspired a hit movie, a Broadway bound musical, and a successful clothing line. In March 1997, the movie *Selena*, was released. The Quintanilla family helped with the movie, which starred

> *Today, Selena still has millions of fans all around the globe.*

Latina actress, Jennifer Lopez. The *Selena* movie helped to launch Lopez's acting career. In March 2000, the musical "Selena Forever" opened in San Antonio's Municipal Auditorium and then headed to Dallas and Corpus Christi. *People* magazine published a commemorative issue of Selena, which sold a record number of copies. This issue ultimately spurred the creation of the magazine *People en Español*. She is still regarded as the *"Queen of Tejano"* by her fans. In 2003, her music is still played on radio stations of every format. Thousands from around the world still flock to Corpus Christi to see her statue, gravesite and the home where she was raised. Her father, Abraham, has continued his entertainment company *Q Productions* in Corpus Christi. He specializes in management, promotions, bookings, and film/video productions. He has guided the ca-

The cast of Selena *is shown here. Jennifer Lopez, who played Selena, is second from the right.*

This memorial in Victoria, Texas honored the one-year anniversary of Selena's death.

reer paths of Los Kumbia Kings, Chris Perez Band, and Mireya. He remains committed to helping young Latin artists develop their own style and sound. After Selena's death, Abraham Quintanilla said he sometimes forgot that his daughter was no longer alive because there were so many daily reminders of her, such as her music on the radio or the fans who approached him and his family and wanted to share their memories. "But then I read something that says 'the late Selena' and reality sets in," he said.

"That is just a wound to our hearts that will always be there."

Selena touched the lives of millions of people. What she accomplished in a short 23 years is often not equalled by many in a lifetime. She is still respected and admired world-wide for her beautiful voice, fierce determination, and eternally happy attitude.

CHRONOLOGY

1971 Born April 16 in Lake Jackson, Texas to mother Marcela and father Abraham Quintanilla

1981 Moves to Corpus Christi, Texas, after her father's restaurant fails; begins singing with the family band

1985 makes her first commercial recording

1987 wins the Tejano Music Awards in San Antonio for best female vocalist and performer of the year

1989 signs with EMI Latin to record Spanish-language music

1991 gives Yolanda Saldívar the unpaid position of founding her fan club

1992 marries Chris Pérez, the band's guitarist, on April 2

1994 receives Grammy for *Selena Live!*; receives an English-language contract from SBK records; August, puts Yolanda in charge of her new business, Selena Etc., Inc.

1995 January to March, the Quintanillas hear rumors that Yolanda is taking money from the business; March 30, Selena tries to discuss financial discrepancies with Yolanda; March 31, Selena is shot by Yolanda Saldívar at the Days Inn in Corpus Christi. She dies at 1:05 P.M. at Memorial Medical Center; April 3, the movie *Don Juan DeMarco*, in which Selena had a small acting part, premieres; EMI releases *Dreaming of You*, an album that Selena was making at the time of her death

FOR FURTHER READING

Jones, Veda Boyd. *Selena.* Philadelphia: Chelsea House, 2000.

Novas, Himilce. *Rembembering Selena.* New York: Tor Books, 1995.

Patoski, Joe Nick. *Selena.* New York: Berkley Publishing Group, 1999.

Richmond, Clint. *Selena: The Phenomenal Life and Tragic Death of the Tejano Music Queen.* New York: Pocket Books, 1995.

Romero, Maritza. *Selena Perez: Queen of Tejano Music.* New York: Powerkids, 1998.

Wheeler, Jill C. *Selena: The Queen of Tejano.* Minneapolis: Abdo, 1996.

On the Web:

Como La Flor: http://www.comolaflor.org

Q-Productions: http://www.q-productions.com/selena.htm

DISCOGRAPHY

1984   *Mis Primeras Grabaciones*
1989   *Selena*
1990   *16 Super Exitos*
        Ven Conmigo
1992   *Entre A Mi Mundo*
1993   *Mis Mejores Canciones: 17 Super Exitos*
        Selena Live!
1994   *12 Super Exitos*
        Amor Prohibido
1995   *Dreaming Of You*
        Las Reinas Del Pueblo

(continued on next page)

INDEX